LOOK INSIDE
CROSS-SECTIONS
TANKS

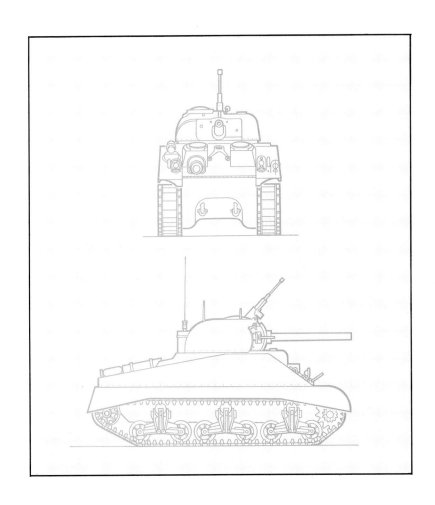

LOOK INSIDE
CROSS-SECTIONS
TANKS

ILLUSTRATED BY
RICHARD CHASEMORE

WRITTEN BY
IAN HARVEY

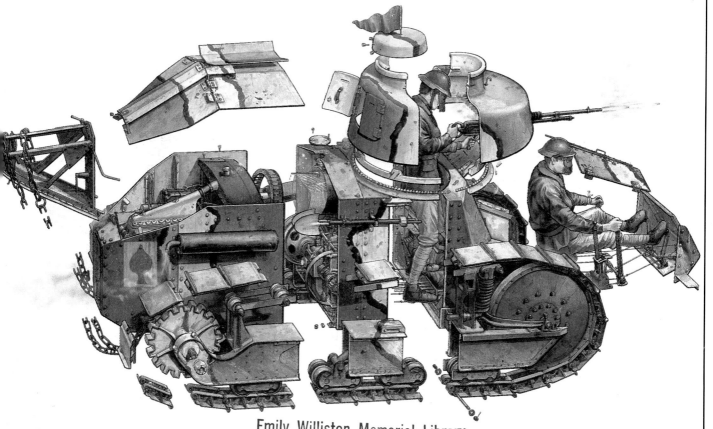

A DK PUBLISHING BOOK

Senior Art Editor Dorian Spencer Davies
Designer Joanne Earl
Senior Editor John C. Miles
Editorial Assistant Nigel Ritchie
U.S. Editor Camela Decaire
Deputy Art Director Miranda Kennedy
Deputy Editorial Director Sophie Mitchell
Production Charlotte Traill
Consultant David Fletcher
The Tank Museum
Bovington, Dorset

First American edition, 1996
2 4 6 8 10 9 7 5 3 1
Published in the United States
by DK Publishing, Inc.,
95 Madison Avenue, New York, New York 10016

**A CIP catalog record is available
from the Library of Congress**

ISBN: 0-7894-0768-X

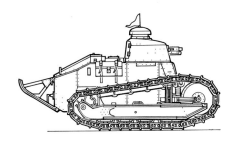

Reproduced by Dot Gradations. Essex
Printed and bound in Belgium by Proost

CONTENTS

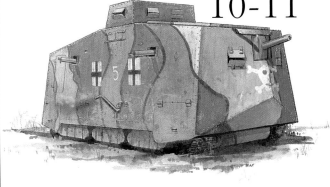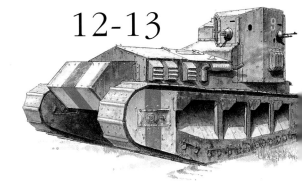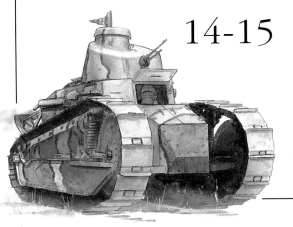

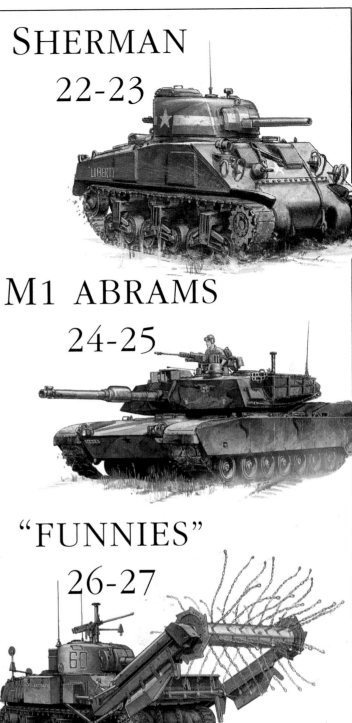
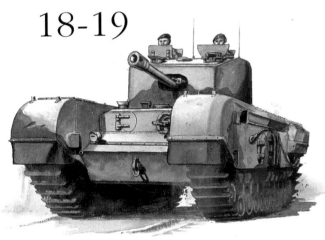

MARK I 1916

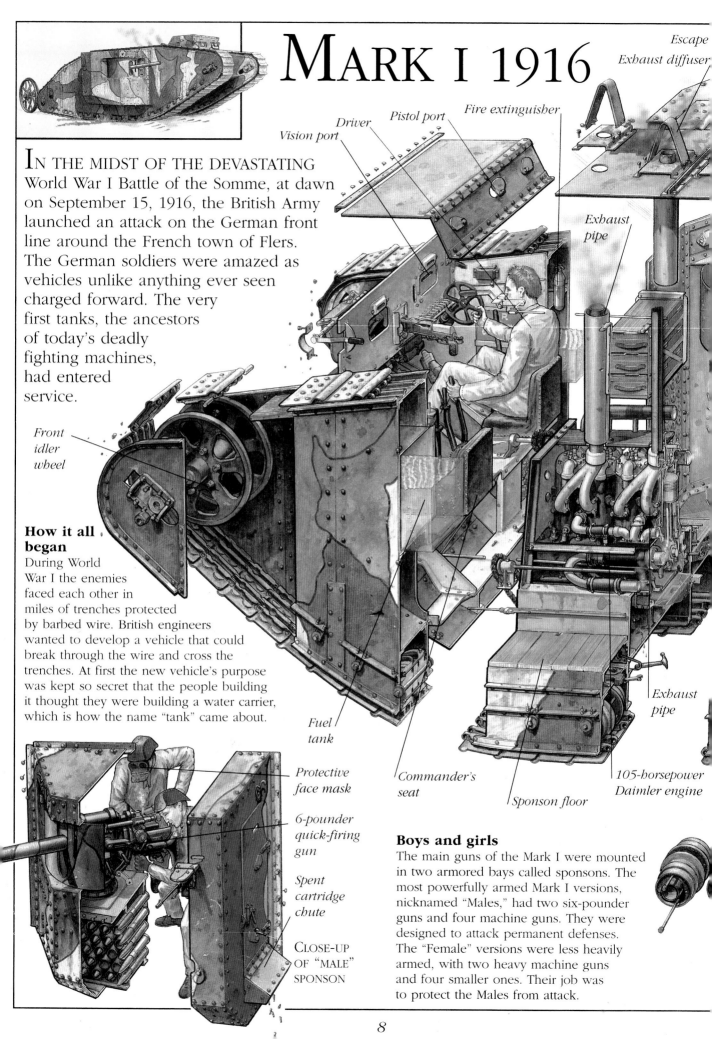

IN THE MIDST OF THE DEVASTATING World War I Battle of the Somme, at dawn on September 15, 1916, the British Army launched an attack on the German front line around the French town of Flers. The German soldiers were amazed as vehicles unlike anything ever seen charged forward. The very first tanks, the ancestors of today's deadly fighting machines, had entered service.

Escape
Exhaust diffuser

Fire extinguisher

Pistol port

Driver

Vision port

Exhaust pipe

Front idler wheel

How it all began

During World War I the enemies faced each other in miles of trenches protected by barbed wire. British engineers wanted to develop a vehicle that could break through the wire and cross the trenches. At first the new vehicle's purpose was kept so secret that the people building it thought they were building a water carrier, which is how the name "tank" came about.

Fuel tank

Commander's seat

Exhaust pipe

105-horsepower Daimler engine

Sponson floor

Protective face mask

6-pounder quick-firing gun

Spent cartridge chute

CLOSE-UP OF "MALE" SPONSON

Boys and girls

The main guns of the Mark I were mounted in two armored bays called sponsons. The most powerfully armed Mark I versions, nicknamed "Males," had two six-pounder guns and four machine guns. They were designed to attack permanent defenses. The "Female" versions were less heavily armed, with two heavy machine guns and four smaller ones. Their job was to protect the Males from attack.

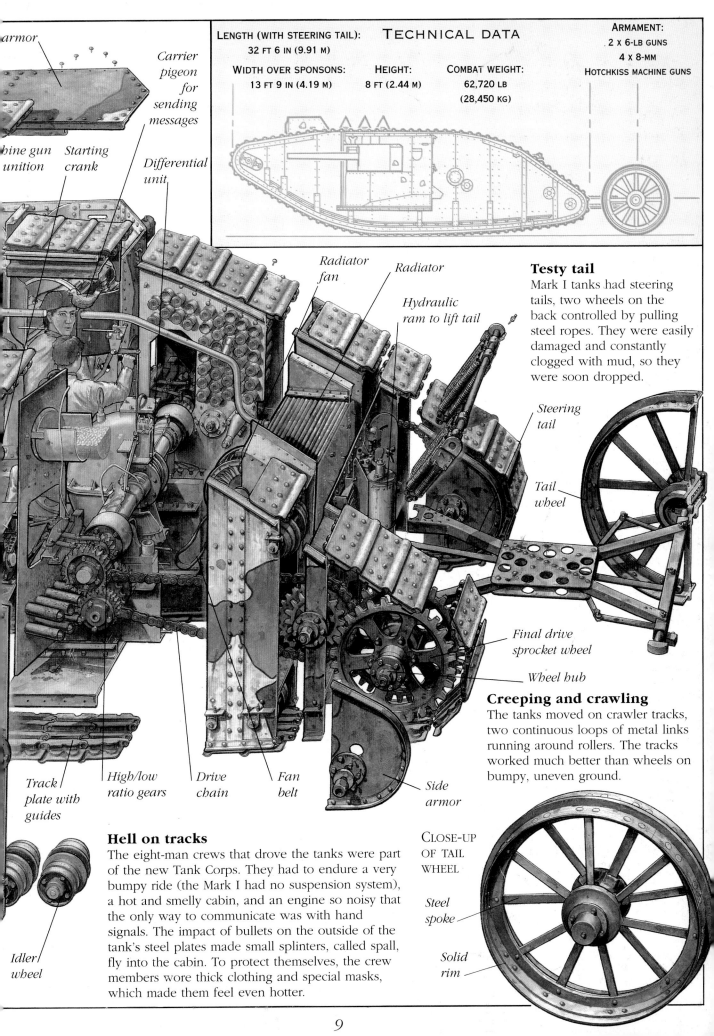

armor

Carrier
pigeon
for
sending
messages

hine gun
unition

Starting
crank

Differential
unit

LENGTH (WITH STEERING TAIL):   TECHNICAL DATA
32 FT 6 IN (9.91 M)

WIDTH OVER SPONSONS: HEIGHT: COMBAT WEIGHT:
13 FT 9 IN (4.19 M)   8 FT (2.44 M)   62,720 LB
                                          (28,450 KG)

ARMAMENT:
2 x 6-LB GUNS
4 x 8-MM
HOTCHKISS MACHINE GUNS

Radiator
fan

Radiator

Hydraulic
ram to lift tail

Testy tail

Mark I tanks had steering
tails, two wheels on the
back controlled by pulling
steel ropes. They were easily
damaged and constantly
clogged with mud, so they
were soon dropped.

Steering
tail

Tail
wheel

Final drive
sprocket wheel

Wheel hub

Creeping and crawling

The tanks moved on crawler tracks,
two continuous loops of metal links
running around rollers. The tracks
worked much better than wheels on
bumpy, uneven ground.

Track
plate with
guides

High/low
ratio gears

Drive
chain

Fan
belt

Side
armor

Hell on tracks

The eight-man crews that drove the tanks were part
of the new Tank Corps. They had to endure a very
bumpy ride (the Mark I had no suspension system),
a hot and smelly cabin, and an engine so noisy that
the only way to communicate was with hand
signals. The impact of bullets on the outside of the
tank's steel plates made small splinters, called spall,
fly into the cabin. To protect themselves, the crew
members wore thick clothing and special masks,
which made them feel even hotter.

CLOSE-UP
OF TAIL
WHEEL

Steel
spoke

Solid
rim

Idler
wheel

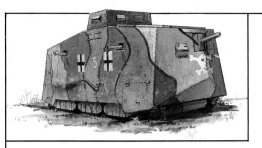

A7V

WHEN THE GERMAN FORCES SAW THE new Allied tanks, they quickly set about making versions of their own. They decided to go giant-sized. In 1917 they began to make the A7V *Sturmpanzerwagen*, which was really a large armored fortress. It carried 18 men and was heavily armed, but it moved slowly and could not climb steep slopes or cross trenches. Nevertheless, on April 24, 1918, military history was made when the first tank battle took place – A7Vs against British Mark IVs (developed versions of the Mark I).

Guns aplenty
In the crowded A7V there was a commander, a driver, and two mechanics, two men manning the main gun, and twelve machine-gunners. Traveling at a top speed of only about 5 mph (9 km/h), the A7V made up for its slowness with lots of firepower. Its main gun was a 57-mm cannon and it had six 7.92-mm machine guns positioned around the sides and at the back. That meant it could fire shells and spray a deadly hail of bullets.

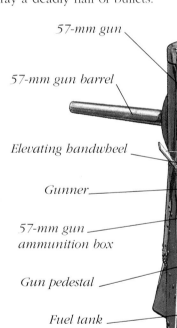

Cupola

Commander

Driver

Steering wheel

Driver's pedal

Roof armor plate

Gun loader

57-mm gun

57-mm gun barrel

Elevating handwheel

Gunner

57-mm gun ammunition box

Gun pedestal

Fuel tank

Front idler wheel

Cross-country clodhopper
The A7V did not travel well over uneven ground. Its tracks were short and didn't rise up at the front like the Allied tank tracks, which meant it could only clear a small slope or a narrow trench. Also, the bottom of the tank was close to the ground and easily got stuck on bumps. To make matters even worse, the tank was very heavy, so its engines overheated and wore out quickly.

Track bogie

Engine radiator

Muffler

Exhaust pipe

Daimler engine

TECHNICAL DATA

LENGTH:	HEIGHT:		ARMAMENT:	WIDTH:
FT 3 IN (8 M)	11 FT 6 IN (3.5 M)		1 X 57-MM GUN	10 FT 6 IN (3.2 M)
			6 X 7.92-MM MACHINE GUNS	

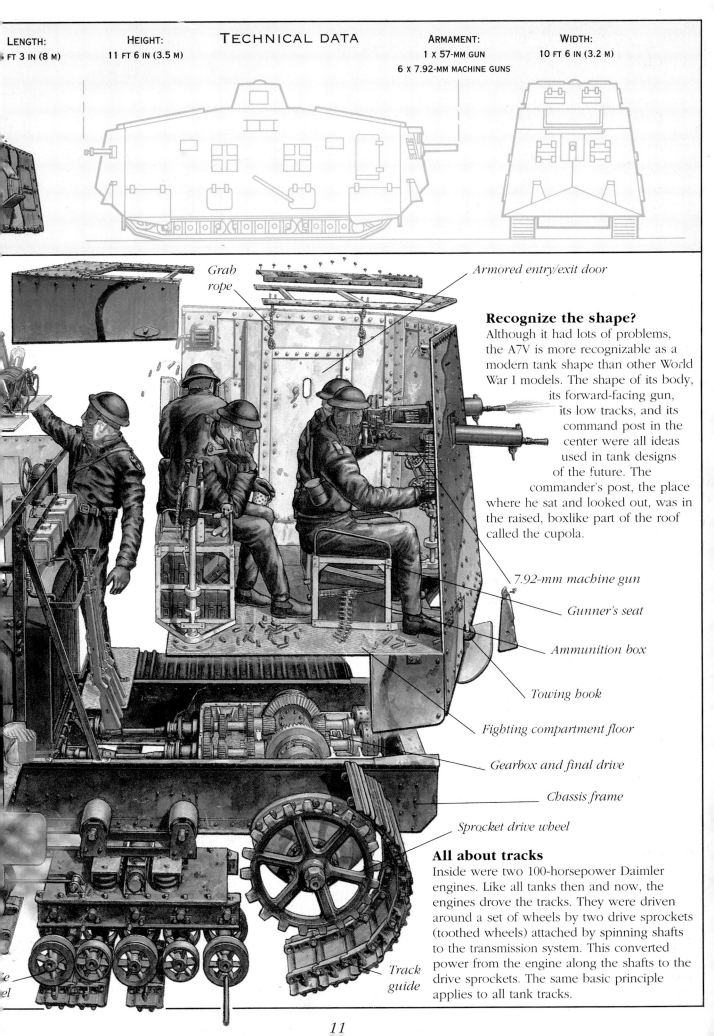

Grab rope

Armored entry/exit door

Recognize the shape?

Although it had lots of problems, the A7V is more recognizable as a modern tank shape than other World War I models. The shape of its body, its forward-facing gun, its low tracks, and its command post in the center were all ideas used in tank designs of the future. The commander's post, the place where he sat and looked out, was in the raised, boxlike part of the roof called the cupola.

7.92-mm machine gun

Gunner's seat

Ammunition box

Towing hook

Fighting compartment floor

Gearbox and final drive

Chassis frame

Sprocket drive wheel

All about tracks

Inside were two 100-horsepower Daimler engines. Like all tanks then and now, the engines drove the tracks. They were driven around a set of wheels by two drive sprockets (toothed wheels) attached by spinning shafts to the transmission system. This converted power from the engine along the shafts to the drive sprockets. The same basic principle applies to all tank tracks.

Track guide

WHIPPET

T HE MARK I TANKS COULD BREAK through a front line of trenches, but they were too slow to go much farther. A lighter, faster tank was needed to penetrate farther behind the front line and do more damage. Officially this new design, the first-ever light tank, was called the Medium Tank Mark A, but it soon became known to everyone as the "Whippet," nicknamed after the lightning-fast whippet breed of dog. Whippets were first used near the end of the war in 1918, when they lived up to their nickname during the Battle of Amiens, managing to get nearly 10 miles (16 km) behind enemy lines.

Turret time
The Whippet was the fi
tank to have a barbette,
raised turret. Although i
could not turn
around, the
tank's crew
could fire machine
guns through gunports
on all sides of it.

Double trouble
At 16 tons (14.2 tonnes) the Whippet was half the weight of a Mark I; it could cruise along at twice a Mark I's speed -- up to 8 mph (13 km/h); and at the front of the tank were two 45-horsepower engines, each one driving a crawler track.

Turning
The Whippet was turned by running one track more quickly than the other, using two clutches and two gearboxes. This required a great deal of skill on the part of the driver – it was like driving two cars at the same time!

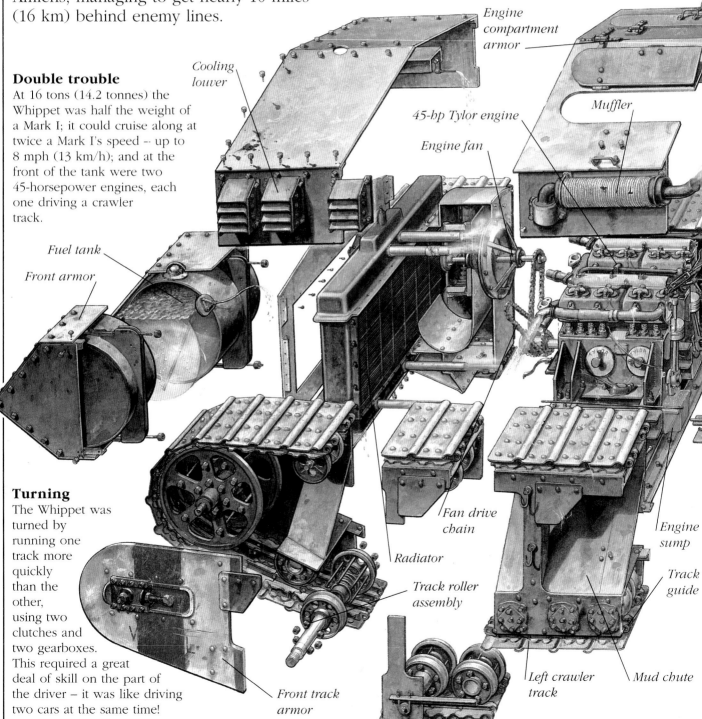

Cooling louver

Engine compartment armor

Muffler

45-hp Tylor engine

Engine fan

Fuel tank

Front armor

Fan drive chain

Engine sump

Radiator

Track guide

Track roller assembly

Left crawler track

Mud chute

Front track armor

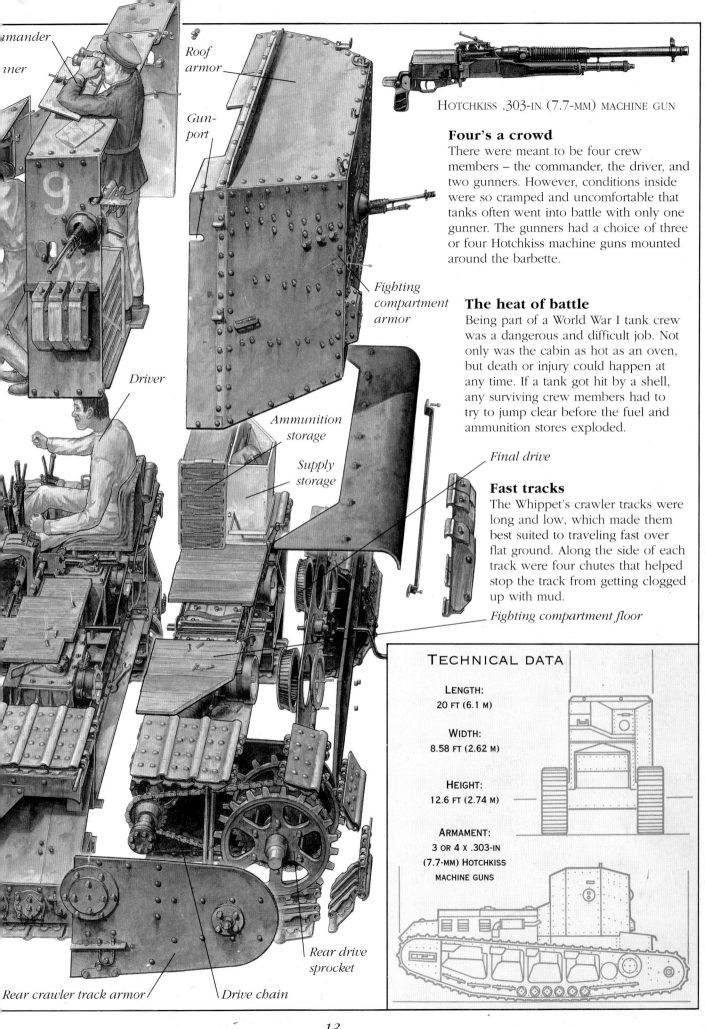

commander
ner

Roof armor

Gun-port

9
A2

HOTCHKISS .303-IN (7.7-MM) MACHINE GUN

Four's a crowd

There were meant to be four crew members – the commander, the driver, and two gunners. However, conditions inside were so cramped and uncomfortable that tanks often went into battle with only one gunner. The gunners had a choice of three or four Hotchkiss machine guns mounted around the barbette.

The heat of battle

Being part of a World War I tank crew was a dangerous and difficult job. Not only was the cabin as hot as an oven, but death or injury could happen at any time. If a tank got hit by a shell, any surviving crew members had to try to jump clear before the fuel and ammunition stores exploded.

Fighting compartment armor

Driver

Ammunition storage

Supply storage

Final drive

Fast tracks

The Whippet's crawler tracks were long and low, which made them best suited to traveling fast over flat ground. Along the side of each track were four chutes that helped stop the track from getting clogged up with mud.

Fighting compartment floor

Rear drive sprocket

Rear crawler track armor

Drive chain

TECHNICAL DATA

LENGTH:
20 FT (6.1 M)

WIDTH:
8.58 FT (2.62 M)

HEIGHT:
12.6 FT (2.74 M)

ARMAMENT:
3 OR 4 X .303-IN
(7.7-MM) HOTCHKISS
MACHINE GUNS

RENAULT FT17

DURING WORLD WAR I THE FRENCH ALSO HAD CLEVER engineers developing tanks. One of their best designs was the Renault FT17, introduced in 1918. It was a light, fast tank originally meant to be used in big groups leading infantry through holes in trench defenses made by bigger tanks. It was also useful for racing ahead to survey the land for the infantry. Because it was light, it wasn't very successful on bumpy ground, but it was ideal for fighting in open spaces. It was so popular that many other countries began to buy it after the war.

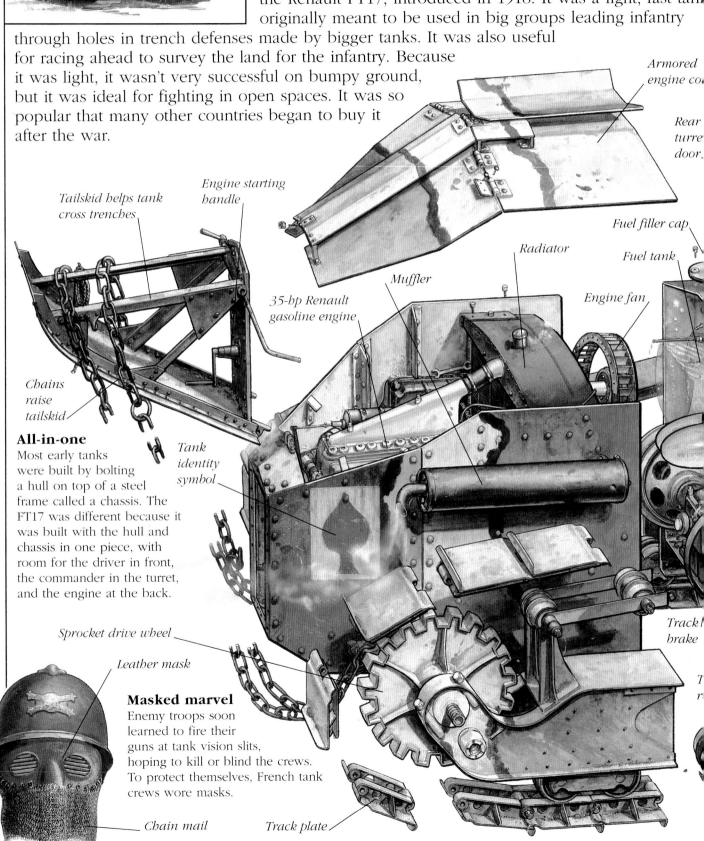

Tailskid helps tank cross trenches

Engine starting handle

Chains raise tailskid

All-in-one
Most early tanks were built by bolting a hull on top of a steel frame called a chassis. The FT17 was different because it was built with the hull and chassis in one piece, with room for the driver in front, the commander in the turret, and the engine at the back.

Tank identity symbol

35-hp Renault gasoline engine

Muffler

Armored engine cover

Rear turret door

Fuel filler cap

Fuel tank

Radiator

Engine fan

Sprocket drive wheel

Leather mask

Masked marvel
Enemy troops soon learned to fire their guns at tank vision slits, hoping to kill or blind the crews. To protect themselves, French tank crews wore masks.

Chain mail

Track plate

Track brake

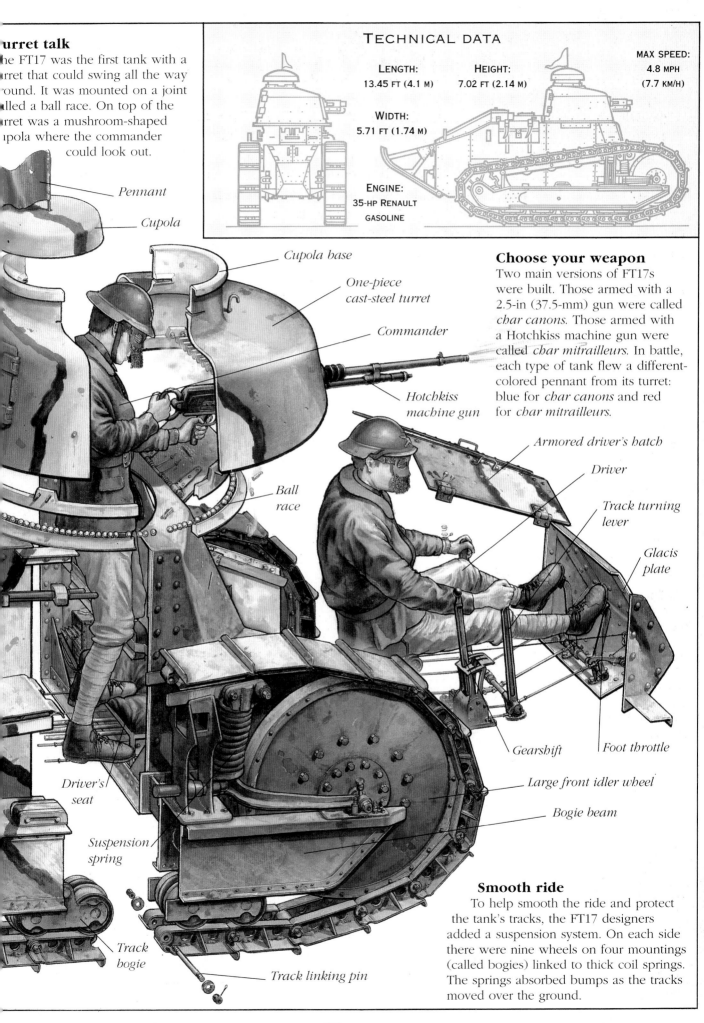

Turret talk

The FT17 was the first tank with a turret that could swing all the way round. It was mounted on a joint called a ball race. On top of the turret was a mushroom-shaped cupola where the commander could look out.

Pennant

Cupola

TECHNICAL DATA

LENGTH:
13.45 FT (4.1 M)

HEIGHT:
7.02 FT (2.14 M)

MAX SPEED:
4.8 MPH
(7.7 KM/H)

WIDTH:
5.71 FT (1.74 M)

ENGINE:
35-HP RENAULT
GASOLINE

Cupola base

One-piece cast-steel turret

Commander

Hotchkiss machine gun

Choose your weapon

Two main versions of FT17s were built. Those armed with a 2.5-in (37.5-mm) gun were called *char canons*. Those armed with a Hotchkiss machine gun were called *char mitrailleurs*. In battle, each type of tank flew a different-colored pennant from its turret: blue for *char canons* and red for *char mitrailleurs*.

Armored driver's hatch

Driver

Track turning lever

Glacis plate

Ball race

Driver's seat

Suspension spring

Track bogie

Track linking pin

Gearshift

Foot throttle

Large front idler wheel

Bogie beam

Smooth ride

To help smooth the ride and protect the tank's tracks, the FT17 designers added a suspension system. On each side there were nine wheels on four mountings (called bogies) linked to thick coil springs. The springs absorbed bumps as the tracks moved over the ground.

RUSSIAN T-34

IN 1939 THE WORLD WENT TO WAR A SECOND TIME and this time the Germans used tanks very effectively in *Blitzkrieg*, or lightning war, strategy. Panzer tanks rolled across Europe and pushed deep into Russia, but even as Russians fell back, they were preparing a surprise for the Germans – the T-34 tank. It was fast and thickly armored, with a gun so powerful and accurate that it could knock out enemy tanks before they got close enough to return fire.

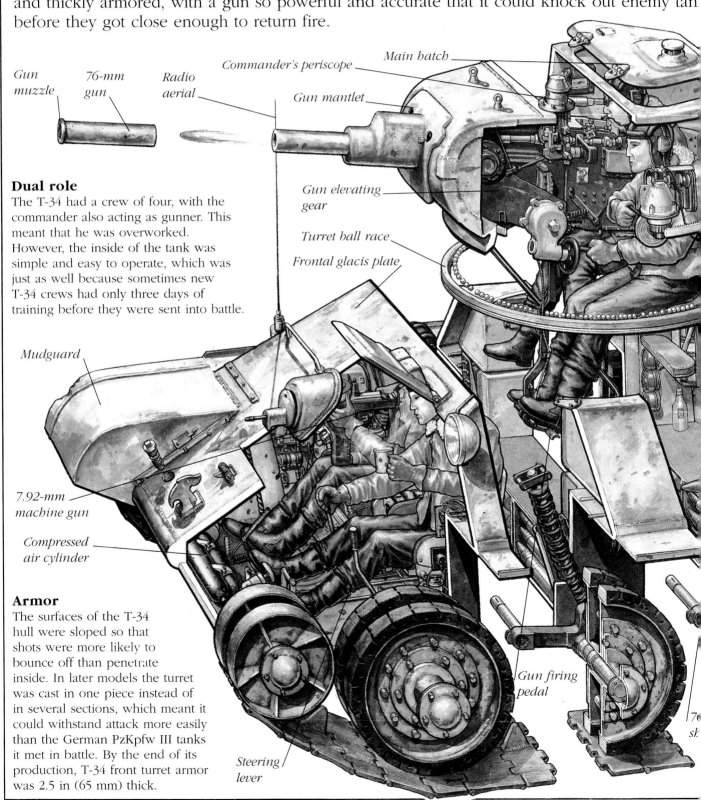

Gun muzzle

76-mm gun

Radio aerial

Commander's periscope

Main hatch

Gun mantlet

Gun elevating gear

Turret ball race

Frontal glacis plate

Mudguard

7.92-mm machine gun

Compressed air cylinder

Gun firing pedal

Steering lever

Dual role

The T-34 had a crew of four, with the commander also acting as gunner. This meant that he was overworked. However, the inside of the tank was simple and easy to operate, which was just as well because sometimes new T-34 crews had only three days of training before they were sent into battle.

Armor

The surfaces of the T-34 hull were sloped so that shots were more likely to bounce off than penetrate inside. In later models the turret was cast in one piece instead of in several sections, which meant it could withstand attack more easily than the German PzKpfw III tanks it met in battle. By the end of its production, T-34 front turret armor was 2.5 in (65 mm) thick.

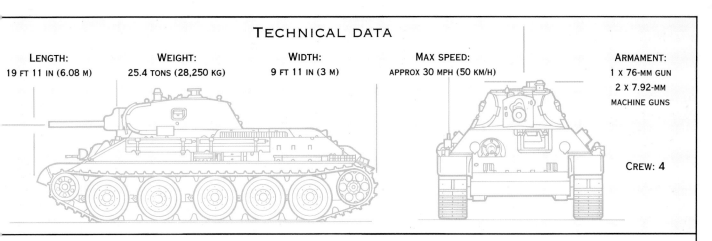

Antifreeze features

The engine ran on diesel fuel, which wouldn't freeze up in the depths of a Russian winter. It had an electric starter motor, and if this didn't work in cold weather, the crew could start the engine using compressed air stored in cylinders at the front of the tank.

Moving along

The first T-34s were built in factories in Leningrad, Kharkov, and Stalingrad. As the Germans advanced toward these places, the Russians dismantled the Leningrad and Kharkov factories piece by piece and moved them to faraway Siberia, where they were rebuilt. They were combined on a site that became known as "Tankograd." The tanks continued to be made at Stalingrad, where they were driven straight off the assembly line into the battle raging nearby.

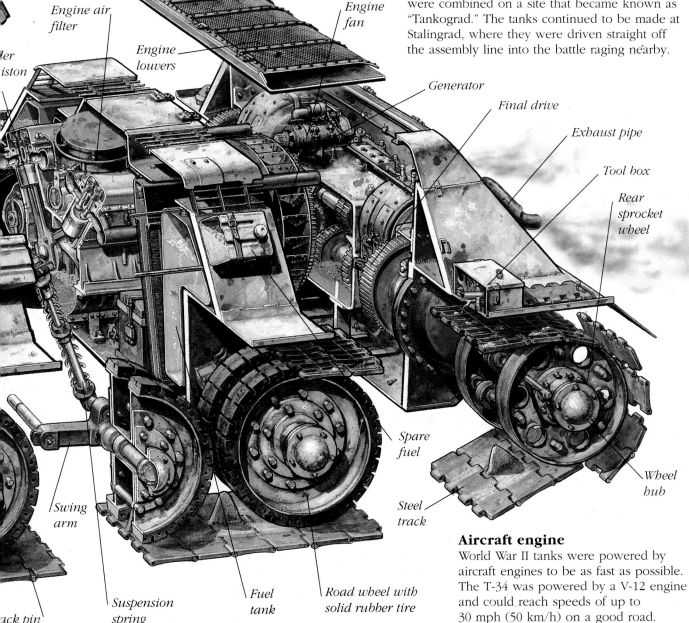

Engine air filter

Engine louvers

Engine fan

Generator

Final drive

Exhaust pipe

Tool box

Rear sprocket wheel

Spare fuel

Wheel hub

Steel track

Swing arm

Suspension spring

Fuel tank

Road wheel with solid rubber tire

Aircraft engine

World War II tanks were powered by aircraft engines to be as fast as possible. The T-34 was powered by a V-12 engine and could reach speeds of up to 30 mph (50 km/h) on a good road.

CHURCHILL

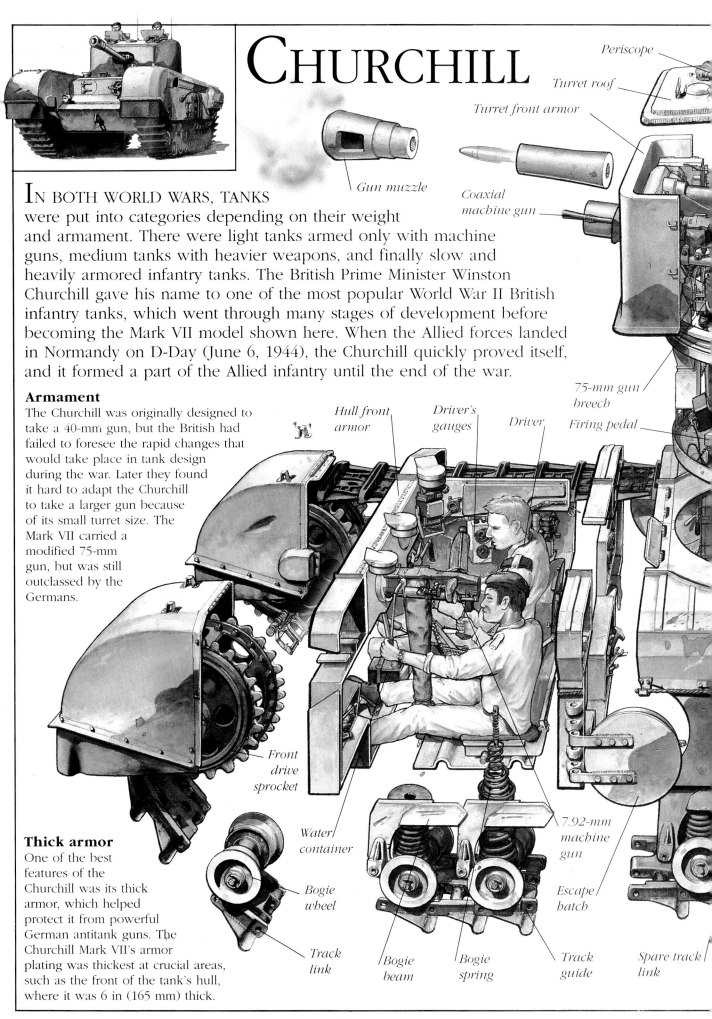

Periscope

Turret roof

Turret front armor

Gun muzzle

Coaxial machine gun

IN BOTH WORLD WARS, TANKS
were put into categories depending on their weight
and armament. There were light tanks armed only with machine
guns, medium tanks with heavier weapons, and finally slow and
heavily armored infantry tanks. The British Prime Minister Winston
Churchill gave his name to one of the most popular World War II British
infantry tanks, which went through many stages of development before
becoming the Mark VII model shown here. When the Allied forces landed
in Normandy on D-Day (June 6, 1944), the Churchill quickly proved itself,
and it formed a part of the Allied infantry until the end of the war.

75-mm gun breech

Armament

The Churchill was originally designed to
take a 40-mm gun, but the British had
failed to foresee the rapid changes that
would take place in tank design
during the war. Later they found
it hard to adapt the Churchill
to take a larger gun because
of its small turret size. The
Mark VII carried a
modified 75-mm
gun, but was still
outclassed by the
Germans.

Hull front armor

Driver's gauges

Driver

Firing pedal

Front drive sprocket

Water container

7.92-mm machine gun

Thick armor

One of the best
features of the
Churchill was its thick
armor, which helped
protect it from powerful
German antitank guns. The
Churchill Mark VII's armor
plating was thickest at crucial areas,
such as the front of the tank's hull,
where it was 6 in (165 mm) thick.

Bogie wheel

Track link

Bogie beam

Bogie spring

Track guide

Escape hatch

Spare track link

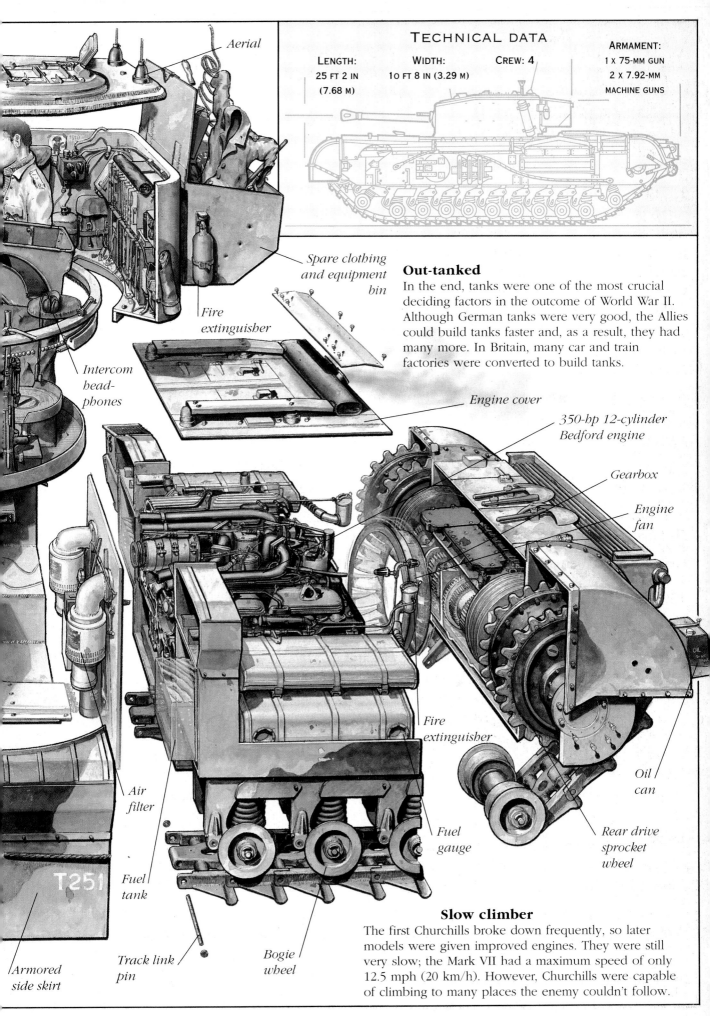

TECHNICAL DATA

LENGTH:	WIDTH:	CREW: 4	ARMAMENT:
25 FT 2 IN	10 FT 8 IN (3.29 M)		1 x 75-MM GUN
(7.68 M)			2 x 7.92-MM
			MACHINE GUNS

Aerial

Spare clothing
and equipment
bin

Fire
extinguisher

Intercom
head-
phones

Engine cover

350-hp 12-cylinder
Bedford engine

Gearbox

Engine
fan

Air
filter

Fire
extinguisher

Oil
can

T251

Fuel
tank

Fuel
gauge

Rear drive
sprocket
wheel

Armored
side skirt

Track link
pin

Bogie
wheel

Out-tanked

In the end, tanks were one of the most crucial
deciding factors in the outcome of World War II.
Although German tanks were very good, the Allies
could build tanks faster and, as a result, they had
many more. In Britain, many car and train
factories were converted to build tanks.

Slow climber

The first Churchills broke down frequently, so later
models were given improved engines. They were still
very slow; the Mark VII had a maximum speed of only
12.5 mph (20 km/h). However, Churchills were capable
of climbing to many places the enemy couldn't follow.

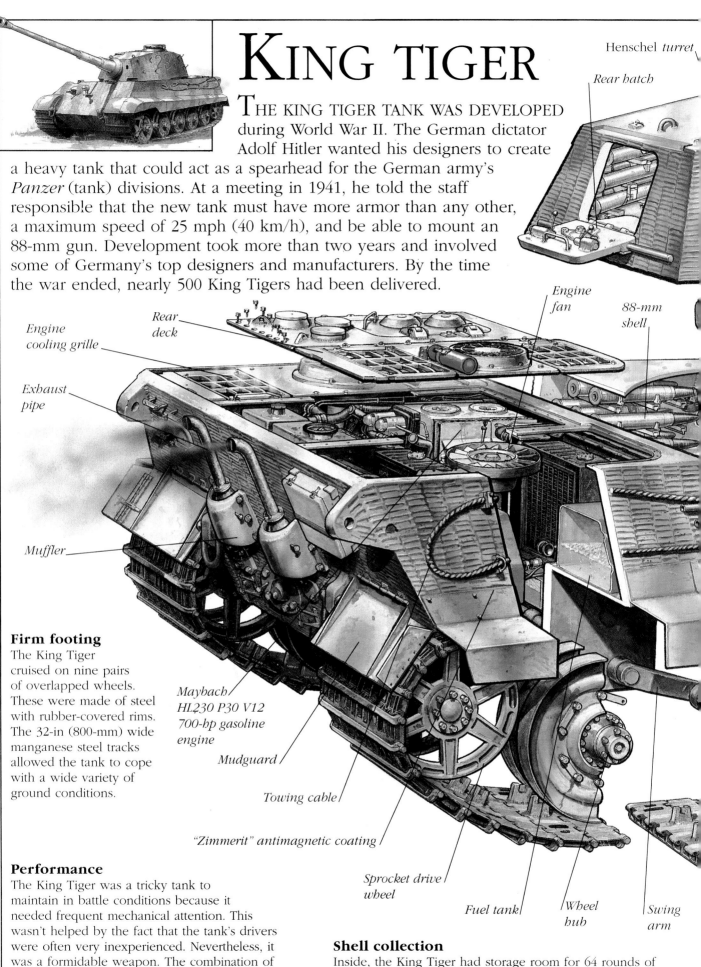

KING TIGER

Henschel *turret*

Rear hatch

THE KING TIGER TANK WAS DEVELOPED during World War II. The German dictator Adolf Hitler wanted his designers to create a heavy tank that could act as a spearhead for the German army's *Panzer* (tank) divisions. At a meeting in 1941, he told the staff responsible that the new tank must have more armor than any other, a maximum speed of 25 mph (40 km/h), and be able to mount an 88-mm gun. Development took more than two years and involved some of Germany's top designers and manufacturers. By the time the war ended, nearly 500 King Tigers had been delivered.

Engine fan

88-mm shell

Rear deck

Engine cooling grille

Exhaust pipe

Muffler

Firm footing
The King Tiger cruised on nine pairs of overlapped wheels. These were made of steel with rubber-covered rims. The 32-in (800-mm) wide manganese steel tracks allowed the tank to cope with a wide variety of ground conditions.

Maybach HL230 P30 V12 700-hp gasoline engine

Mudguard

Towing cable

"Zimmerit" antimagnetic coating

Sprocket drive wheel

Fuel tank

Wheel hub

Swing arm

Performance
The King Tiger was a tricky tank to maintain in battle conditions because it needed frequent mechanical attention. This wasn't helped by the fact that the tank's drivers were often very inexperienced. Nevertheless, it was a formidable weapon. The combination of its 88-mm gun and thick armor made it very difficult for Allied forces to knock out.

Shell collection
Inside, the King Tiger had storage room for 64 rounds of 88-mm ammunition. Some of the rounds were stowed in armore[d] bins in the sides of the tank, and others inside the turret.

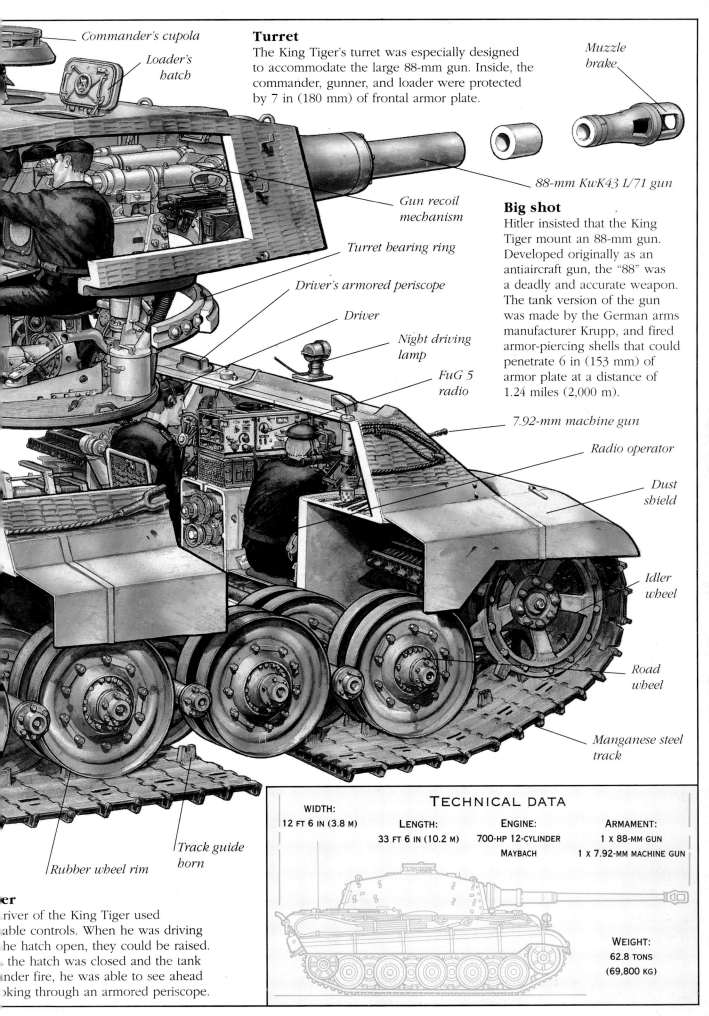

- Commander's cupola
- Loader's hatch

Turret

The King Tiger's turret was especially designed to accommodate the large 88-mm gun. Inside, the commander, gunner, and loader were protected by 7 in (180 mm) of frontal armor plate.

- Muzzle brake

- Gun recoil mechanism

- 88-mm KwK43 L/71 gun

Big shot

Hitler insisted that the King Tiger mount an 88-mm gun. Developed originally as an antiaircraft gun, the "88" was a deadly and accurate weapon. The tank version of the gun was made by the German arms manufacturer Krupp, and fired armor-piercing shells that could penetrate 6 in (153 mm) of armor plate at a distance of 1.24 miles (2,000 m).

- Turret bearing ring
- Driver's armored periscope
- Driver
- Night driving lamp
- FuG 5 radio
- 7.92-mm machine gun
- Radio operator
- Dust shield
- Idler wheel
- Road wheel
- Manganese steel track
- Rubber wheel rim
- Track guide horn

...er

...river of the King Tiger used ...able controls. When he was driving ...e hatch open, they could be raised. ... the hatch was closed and the tank ...nder fire, he was able to see ahead ...oking through an armored periscope.

TECHNICAL DATA			
WIDTH: 12 FT 6 IN (3.8 M)	**LENGTH:** 33 FT 6 IN (10.2 M)	**ENGINE:** 700-HP 12-CYLINDER MAYBACH	**ARMAMENT:** 1 X 88-MM GUN 1 X 7.92-MM MACHINE GUN
			WEIGHT: 62.8 TONS (69,800 KG)

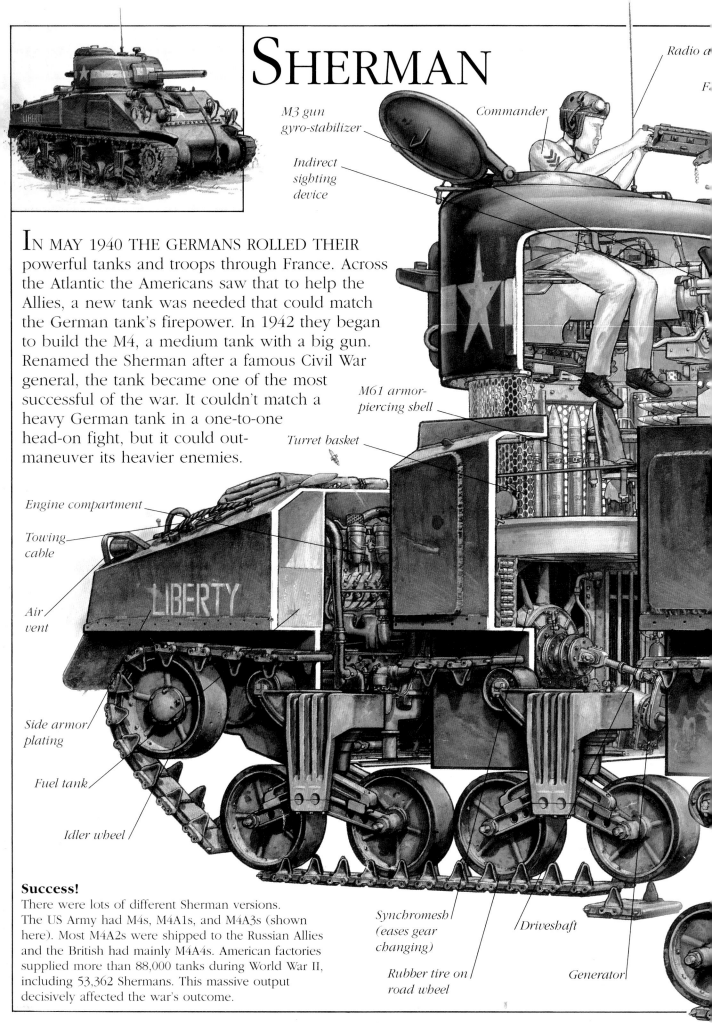

SHERMAN

M3 gun gyro-stabilizer

Indirect sighting device

Commander

Radio a...

F...

IN MAY 1940 THE GERMANS ROLLED THEIR powerful tanks and troops through France. Across the Atlantic the Americans saw that to help the Allies, a new tank was needed that could match the German tank's firepower. In 1942 they began to build the M4, a medium tank with a big gun. Renamed the Sherman after a famous Civil War general, the tank became one of the most successful of the war. It couldn't match a heavy German tank in a one-to-one head-on fight, but it could out-maneuver its heavier enemies.

M61 armor-piercing shell

Turret basket

Engine compartment

Towing cable

Air vent

Side armor plating

Fuel tank

Idler wheel

LIBERTY

Synchromesh (eases gear changing)

Driveshaft

Rubber tire on road wheel

Generator

Success!

There were lots of different Sherman versions. The US Army had M4s, M4A1s, and M4A3s (shown here). Most M4A2s were shipped to the Russian Allies and the British had mainly M4A4s. American factories supplied more than 88,000 tanks during World War II, including 53,362 Shermans. This massive output decisively affected the war's outcome.

...man guns

...ans were fitted with different types of guns that could fire different ... of shells. Versions with 75-mm guns could not penetrate the front of ...vy German tank, but they were fast enough to get around to attack ...ss protected sides. The British upgraded their Shermans with 76-mm ...These were higher velocity, which meant they propelled shells out ...quickly. The faster a shell, the better it is at penetrating metal. The upgraded Shermans were called Fireflies.

Browning .30-cal machine gun

Gun mantlet

75-mm M3 gun

Gun barrel

Co-axial Browning .30-cal machine gun

Gun muzzle

Leather helmet

Driver

Steering lever

Codriver/ machine-gunner

Glacis plate (frontal armor)

Mud-guard

Power train (final drive and brake system)

Guide horn

Towing ring

Road wheel bogie (suspension)

Road wheel

Steel track

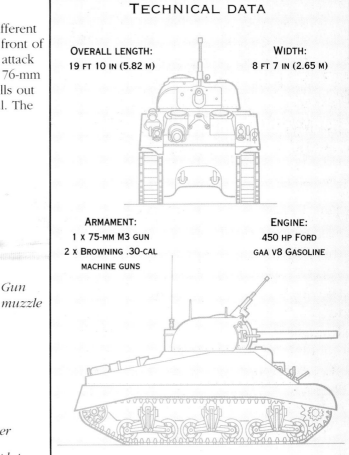

TECHNICAL DATA

OVERALL LENGTH:
19 FT 10 IN (5.82 M)

WIDTH:
8 FT 7 IN (2.65 M)

ARMAMENT:
1 x 75-MM M3 GUN
2 x BROWNING .30-CAL MACHINE GUNS

ENGINE:
450 HP FORD GAA V8 GASOLINE

Clever but confusing

Inside the Sherman was an advanced hydraulic motor called a gyro-stabilizer. This kept the main gun aimed levelly at a specific target when the tank was on the move, even when it went over a bump. Unfortunately it was complicated to use, so gunners often went into battle without bothering to switch it on.

Adding to armor

The Sherman armor plating was thin and couldn't withstand very many direct hits. To improve this some models had metal frames filled with sandbags around the outside of the hull.

Throat microphone

Leather helmet

Look who's talking

Like other World War II tanks, the Sherman had a communications system so the commander could talk to his base. There were "interphones" inside so that crew members could talk to each other.

M1 ABRAMS

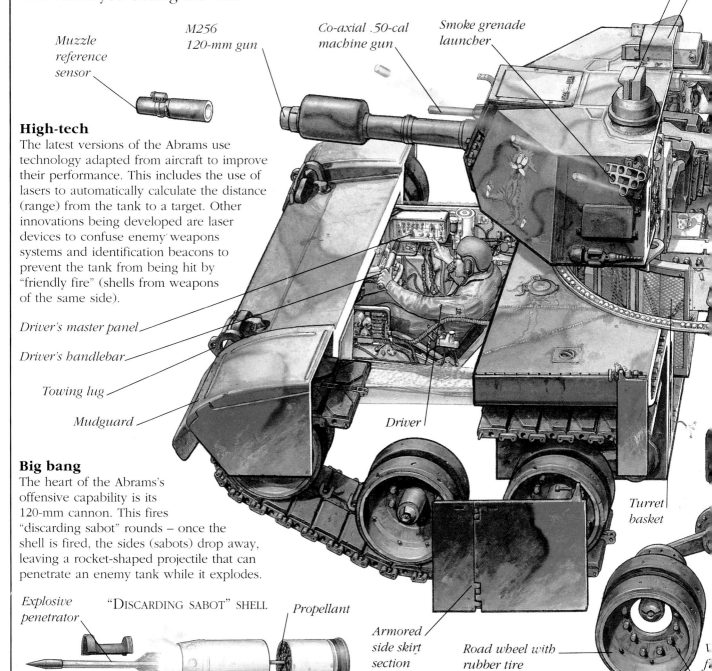

TANKS HAVE COME A LONG WAY SINCE THE end of World War II. Now they have computer and laser technology, much better armor, and a new, sleek outline. Their crews are much safer and more comfortable, a far cry from the stifling heat and overcrowded conditions endured in the experimental days of early tanks. Now designers spend years – and huge amounts of money – designing new tanks. An example is the American M1 Abrams, which took more than a decade to develop. It was first delivered to the US Army in 1980, and will probably be used into the 21st century. It was used in combat during the 1991 Gulf War to destroy more than 2,000 enemy tanks. Amazingly, not a single M1 was destroyed during the war.

Command .50-cal machine g

Gun

Gunner's primary sight

Thermal viewer

Muzzle reference sensor

M256 120-mm gun

Co-axial .50-cal machine gun

Smoke grenade launcher

High-tech
The latest versions of the Abrams use technology adapted from aircraft to improve their performance. This includes the use of lasers to automatically calculate the distance (range) from the tank to a target. Other innovations being developed are laser devices to confuse enemy weapons systems and identification beacons to prevent the tank from being hit by "friendly fire" (shells from weapons of the same side).

Driver's master panel

Driver's handlebar

Towing lug

Mudguard

Driver

Big bang
The heart of the Abrams's offensive capability is its 120-mm cannon. This fires "discarding sabot" rounds – once the shell is fired, the sides (sabots) drop away, leaving a rocket-shaped projectile that can penetrate an enemy tank while it explodes.

Turret basket

Explosive penetrator

"DISCARDING SABOT" SHELL

Propellant

Armored side skirt section

Road wheel with rubber tire

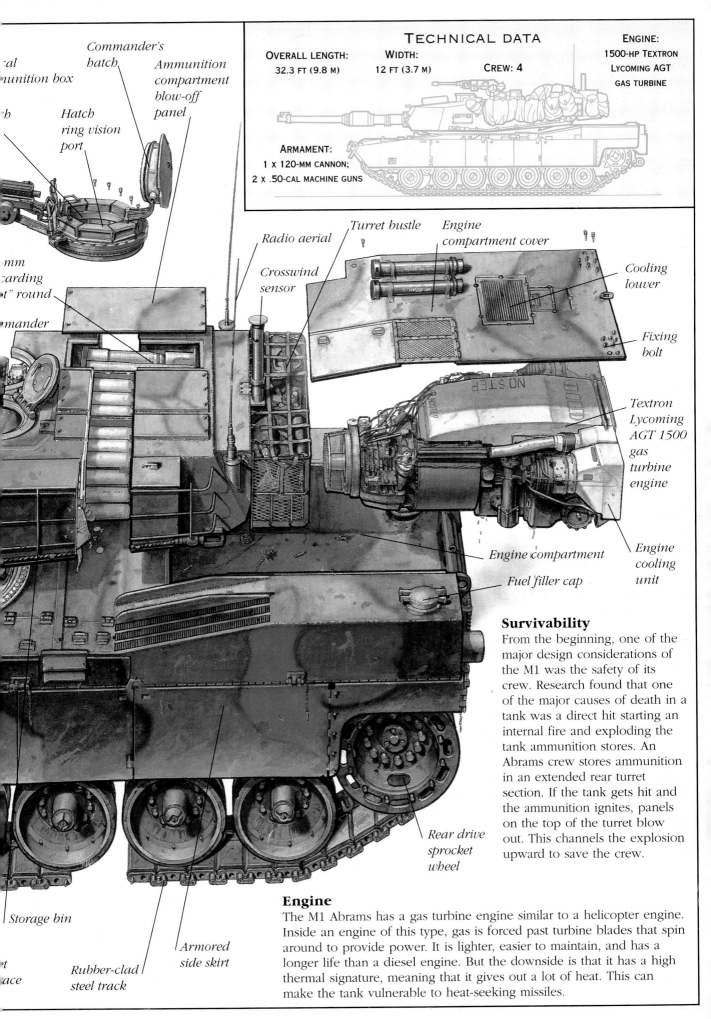

TECHNICAL DATA

OVERALL LENGTH: 32.3 FT (9.8 M)

WIDTH: 12 FT (3.7 M)

CREW: 4

ENGINE: 1500-HP TEXTRON LYCOMING AGT GAS TURBINE

ARMAMENT:
1 x 120-MM CANNON;
2 x .50-CAL MACHINE GUNS

Commander's hatch

Ammunition compartment blow-off panel

...cal ...munition box

...h

Hatch ring vision port

...mm ...carding ...t" round

...mander

Radio aerial

Crosswind sensor

Turret bustle

Engine compartment cover

Cooling louver

Fixing bolt

Textron Lycoming AGT 1500 gas turbine engine

Engine compartment

Engine cooling unit

Fuel filler cap

Rear drive sprocket wheel

Storage bin

Rubber-clad steel track

Armored side skirt

Survivability

From the beginning, one of the major design considerations of the M1 was the safety of its crew. Research found that one of the major causes of death in a tank was a direct hit starting an internal fire and exploding the tank ammunition stores. An Abrams crew stores ammunition in an extended rear turret section. If the tank gets hit and the ammunition ignites, panels on the top of the turret blow out. This channels the explosion upward to save the crew.

Engine

The M1 Abrams has a gas turbine engine similar to a helicopter engine. Inside an engine of this type, gas is forced past turbine blades that spin around to provide power. It is lighter, easier to maintain, and has a longer life than a diesel engine. But the downside is that it has a high thermal signature, meaning that it gives out a lot of heat. This can make the tank vulnerable to heat-seeking missiles.

"FUNNIES"

*The Churchill's bridge wasn't mea[n]
be permanent, but it could be use[d]
engineers built a more solid versio[n].*

Dᴜʀɪɴɢ ᴡᴏʀʟᴅ ᴡᴀʀ ɪɪ, ᴛʜᴇ ᴛᴀɴᴋ ᴡᴀs ʙᴀsɪᴄᴀʟʟʏ ᴜsᴇᴅ
as a mobile armored platform to carry a big gun, either as
an antitank weapon or for helping the infantry. However,
occasionally tanks were needed for other jobs and, since there
was no time to wait for new designs, existing tanks had to be
adapted by engineers. The Sherman and the
Churchill provided most of the
variations, nicknamed "Funnies."
Here are a few examples.

CHURCHILL BRIDGELAYER

*Huge arm swung
bridge into place*

Wide water
World War II tanks
worked best in flat,
open countryside.
Tactics became much more
difficult where there were
hedges or woods, streams
or rivers. An ordinary tank
could be stuck if it came to
a river that was too wide
and deep to cross. That's
when a bridgelaying tank
came in handy.

Bridging the gap
The Churchill Bridgelay[er]
was a standard Churchil[l]
with the turret removed
its place was a
30-ft (9.14-m) br[idge]
that could be
launched forw[ard]
on a powerf[ul]
hinged arn[]

Counterweight

CHURCHILL "CROCODILE" FLAMETHROWER TANK

Difficult pills
German army engineers were good at
building strong defensive positions. All
along the northern French coast they
built strong, concrete pillboxes so they
could fire on the Allies while staying
under cover themselves.

*Turret and hull
looked like an
ordinary Churchill*

Fiery firepower
The British developed the Churchill as a flam[e]
throwing tank that was succesfully able to att[ack]
these obstacles. In addition to its normal gun[,]
tank had a flame gun mounted at the front. A[t]
back was an armored trailer
containing 480 gallons
(1,818 liters) of flame fuel.

*Armored trailer
contained flame fuel*

*The burning fu[el]
was forced out
flame gun by
nitrogen gas u[nder]
pressure*

Flaming jet could reach 80 yards (75 m)

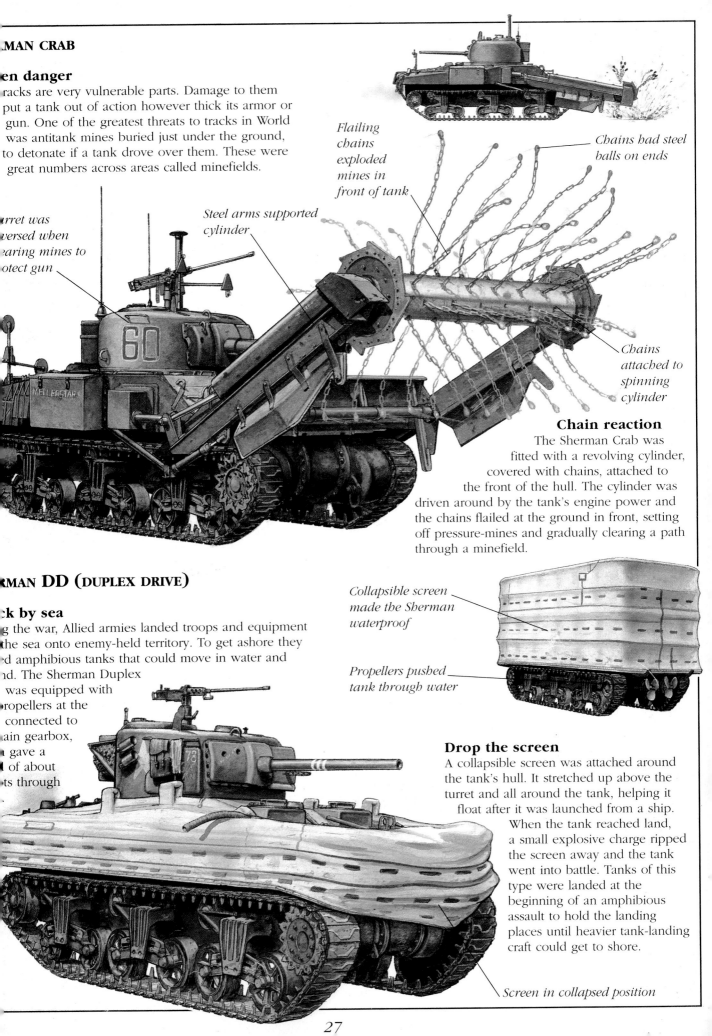

...MAN CRAB

...en danger

...racks are very vulnerable parts. Damage to them ...put a tank out of action however thick its armor or ...gun. One of the greatest threats to tracks in World ...was antitank mines buried just under the ground, ...to detonate if a tank drove over them. These were ...great numbers across areas called minefields.

Flailing chains exploded mines in front of tank

Chains had steel balls on ends

Steel arms supported cylinder

...rret was ...versed when ...earing mines to ...otect gun

60

MELLERSTAIN

Chains attached to spinning cylinder

Chain reaction

The Sherman Crab was fitted with a revolving cylinder, covered with chains, attached to the front of the hull. The cylinder was driven around by the tank's engine power and the chains flailed at the ground in front, setting off pressure-mines and gradually clearing a path through a minefield.

...RMAN DD (DUPLEX DRIVE)

...k by sea

...g the war, Allied armies landed troops and equipment ...the sea onto enemy-held territory. To get ashore they ...d amphibious tanks that could move in water and ...nd. The Sherman Duplex ...was equipped with ...ropellers at the ...connected to ...ain gearbox, ...gave a ...l of about ...ts through

Collapsible screen made the Sherman waterproof

Propellers pushed tank through water

Drop the screen

A collapsible screen was attached around the tank's hull. It stretched up above the turret and all around the tank, helping it float after it was launched from a ship. When the tank reached land, a small explosive charge ripped the screen away and the tank went into battle. Tanks of this type were landed at the beginning of an amphibious assault to hold the landing places until heavier tank-landing craft could get to shore.

Screen in collapsed position

GLOSSARY

Ammunition
Shells and bullets stored in a tank and loaded into its guns during battle.

Amphibious tank
A tank that can travel through water as well as on land. This is useful when armies must make an amphibious landing – landing troops from ships onto land.

Antitank mine
Explosive charge buried beneath the ground and set off by the pressure of a tank driving over it.

Armament
All the different types of guns on board a tank.

Armor
Thick steel plating that helps protect a tank from bullets and shells. Its thickness varies on different tank types.

Barbette
A small turret raised above the body, used in early tanks before revolving turrets were developed.

Basket
A structure inside the hull hanging down below the turret and revolving around with it. The turret crew members sit in the basket.

Blitzkrieg
The German World War II tactic of sending tank divisions racing into enemy territory to split up the enemy forces. Infantry followed the tanks in armored vehicles to provide close support.

Bogies
Wheel mountings that link the wheels of a tank. They help support the weight of the tank's body.

Bridgelayer
A tank carrying a folded-up bridge. It can extend the bridge and lower it down over an obstacle, such as a river. Later, the tank can come back and pick up its bridge to use again.

Bustle
The overhanging back part of a tank turret, usually used to store ammunition or radio equipment.

Caliber
The diameter of a shell that can be fired by a gun. For instance, an 88-mm gun can fire a shell that is 88-mm across.

Chassis
The frame on which a tank body is fixed.

Cupola
An extra section raised above a tank turret, where the commander can look out.

Drive sprocket
A toothed wheel that is turned around by the power of an engine. As it moves, it drives a tank crawler track around.

Bridge center section

Bridge erected hydraulic ram

Fascine
A large roll of brushwood wrapped in wire. Some tanks can carry these and drop them into ditches. The fascines fill up the ditches so that the tanks can drive across them.

Gasoline engine
An engine in which a fuel and air mixture is burned, making gases that push pistons up and down, generating power. Diesel engines need diesel fuel instead of gasoline to make them work.

Gas turbine engine
An engine in which gas is forced past turbine blades, making them spin around to generate power.

Grousers
Metal plates bolted on top of tank tracks to give them extra grip on slippery surfaces such as snow and mud.

Gun emplacement
A building or structur built of sandbags whe gun crew can shelter, aiming guns at the er Tanks are used to de: gun emplacements.

Gyro-stabilizer
A hydraulically powe motor that keeps a g pointed levelly at a t even when its tank is the move.

Hatch
A mini-door for gettir and out of a tank or seeing outside.

Hull
The main body of a t above the tracks. Diff types of tanks have different-shaped hulls

Idler
A wheel inside one e of a tank track. It tur freely as the track mc around.

Infantry
Army foot soldiers. Du both world wars, tank and infantry worked together on the battlef

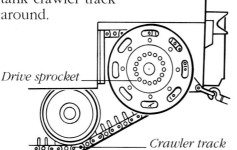

Drive sprocket

Crawler track

Machine gun
A gun that shoots a continuous stream of bullets in one firing.

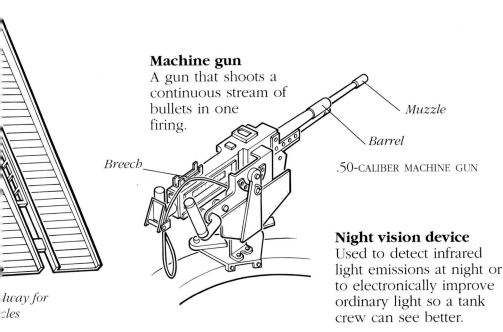

Muzzle

Barrel

Breech

.50-CALIBER MACHINE GUN

...way for ...les

...try tank
...w and heavily ...red tank used to ...t infantry soldiers.

...red
...f a ray of light that ...be seen by the ...n eye. Objects give ...frared rays; the ...er they are, the ...they give off. ...onic tank equipment ...etect infrared light ...pot a hiding enemy.

...phones
...ment crew ...ers use to talk to ...other inside a tank.

...row beam of light ...an be accurately ...ed at a target to ...int it and measure ...tance from a tank.

...tank
...ntweight, fast tank ...l only with machine

...ers
...above a tank's ...e compartment that ...gine heat escape.

Medium tank
A tank armed with a medium-sized gun and machine guns.

Muzzle brake
A part fitted to the muzzle (front) of a gun. When a shell is fired, gases trail out behind it. The brake deflects the gases away from the gun to reduce the gun's recoil (backward jolt).

Muzzle velocity
The speed of a shell or a bullet as it leaves the muzzle of a gun. It is measured in feet or meters per second.

Night vision device
Used to detect infrared light emissions at night or to electronically improve ordinary light so a tank crew can see better.

Panzers
The German word for armor. It came to mean German tanks and also German tank divisions during World War II.

Periscope
Optical device that a crew member can use for seeing outside a tank while sitting inside in safety.

Pistol ports
Small plugged openings along the sides of a tank. When unplugged, crew members can fire revolvers through them to defend themselves.

Range
A word used in three different ways: how far a gun can fire, the distance between a gun and its target, and the distance a tank can travel before it runs out of fuel.

Return rollers
Small wheels that support the upper part of a tank track.

Tracks
Continuous loops of metal links running around rollers on either side of a tank.

Transmission
The parts of a tank that transfer power from the engine to the tracks.

Traverse
The distance a gun can swing from side to side when it is mounted on a tank turret. Also, the distance a turret can rotate around.

Trenches
Long ditches dug across the battlefields of World War I. Troops sheltered in them, protected by barbed wire and mounds of sloping earth called parapets.

Turret
The top part of a tank that holds a big gun. It usually rotates.

M1 ABRAMS TANK

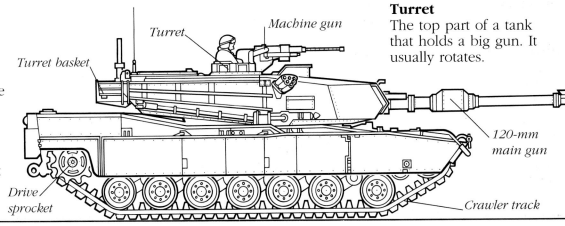

Turret

Machine gun

Turret basket

120-mm main gun

Drive sprocket

Crawler track

29

INDEX

A

A7V *Sturmpanzerwagen,*
10-11
Abrams, 24-25
American tanks, 22-23,
24-25, 27
amphibious tanks, 27, 28
antitank mines, 27, 28
armor, 16, 18, 23, 28
armor-piercing shells, 21

B

ball race, 15
barbette, 12, 28
bogies, 15
bridge, 26
British tanks, 8-9, 12-13,
18-19, 26

C

char canon, 15
char mitrailleur, 15
chassis, 14, 28
Churchill
Bridgelayer, 26
"Crocodile"
flamethrower, 26
Mark VII, 18-19
chutes, 13
commander,
A7V, 10, 11
Renault FT17, 15
T-34, 16
Whippet, 13
communications system,
23
crawler tracks *see* tracks
crew
A7V, 10
Mark I, 9
safety of, 25
T-34, 16

Whippet, 13
cupola, 11, 15, 28

D

"discarding sabot" rounds,
24

E

engine
45-horsepower, 12
100-horsepower
Daimler, 11
diesel, 17, 29
gasoline, 29
gas turbine, 25, 28
V-12, 17

F

"Fireflies," 23
flame gun, 26
French tanks, 14-15
friendly fire, 24
"Funnies," 26-27

G

German tanks, 10-11,
20-21
guns
7.92-mm, 10
37.5-mm, 15
40-mm, 18
57-mm, 10
75-mm, 18, 23
88-mm, 20, 21
105-mm, 24
machine guns, 8, 13,
15, 29
six-pounders, 8
gyro-stabilizer, 23, 28

H

Hotchkiss machine gun,
13, 15
hull, 14, 16, 28

I

infantry tank, 18, 28
interphones, 23, 29

K

King Tiger, 20-21

L

lasers, 24, 29
light tanks, 12, 14, 18, 29

M

Mark I, 8-9
mask, 14
Medium Tank Mark A,
12-13
medium tanks, 16, 18, 29

R

range, 24, 29
Renault FT17, 14-15
Russian tanks, 16-17

S

Sherman
Crab, 27
DD Duplex Drive, 27
M4A3, 22-23
spall, 9

speed
A7V, 10
Churchill Mark VII
King Tiger, 20
T-34, 17
Whippet, 12
sponsons, 8
steering, 12, 21
suspension system, 15

T

T-34, 16-17
tail wheels, 9
tank
main types of, 18
origin of name, 8
Tank Corps, 9
"Tankograd," 17
tracks, 11, 29
A7V, 10
King Tiger, 20
Mark I, 9
Whippet, 13
transmission system, 1
29
trenches, 8, 29
turret, 15, 29
FT17, 15
King Tiger, 21
T-34, 16
Whippet, 12

W

Whippet, 12-13

Acknowledgment

DK would like to thank the
following people who help
with the preparation of this

Gary Biggin for line artworks
Lynn Bresler for the index
Constance Novis for editorial s
Paul Wood for DTP design